THE
Louisa May Alcott
COOKBOOK

THE
Louisa May Alcott
COOKBOOK

COMPILED BY

GRETCHEN ANDERSON

ILLUSTRATED BY

KAREN MILONE

LITTLE, BROWN AND COMPANY
BOSTON TORONTO

FIRST EDITION

The excerpts from *Little Women* and *Little Men* in this book are
taken from the 1915 and 1901 editions respectively, published by
Little, Brown and Company, Boston, Massachusetts.

Library of Congress Cataloging in Publication Data
Anderson, Gretchen
    The Louisa May Alcott cookbook.

    Bibliography; p.
    Includes index
    Summary; Recipes based on the dishes mentioned in
"Little Women" and "Little Men" and recreated from
nineteenth-century cookbooks by the nine-year-old
author.
    1. Cookery, American—Juvenile literature.
2. Alcott, Louisa May, 1832–1888—Juvenile literature.
3. Children's writings. [1. Cookery, American.
2. Alcott, Louisa May, 1832–1888. 3. Children's
writings]   I. Milone-Dugan, Karen, ill.   II. Title.
TX715.A5663   1985   641.5973   85-5196
ISBN 0-316-03951-9

BP

Published simultaneously in Canada
by Little, Brown & Company (Canada) Limited

PRINTED IN THE UNITED STATES OF AMERICA

To Mrs. Beloff, my teacher and friend,
who encouraged me when I doubted,
yet never doubted me when I was discouraged

G.A.

To my parents—who gave me the love and
encouragement to find worlds under my pencil

K.M.

Contents

To the Reader   ix
Louisa May Alcott   xi

FROM
Little Women

The True Spirit of Christmas   3
   Buckwheat Cakes   4
   Muffins   6
   Farina Gruel   7
A Gift from Mr. Laurence   9
   Bonbons   10
   Pound Cake   12
   Mouth-watering Chocolate Glaze   14
The Pickwick Portfolio   17
   Squash   18
Marmee's Breakfast   21
   Omelet   22
   Baking Powder Biscuits   24
Jo's Dinner Party   27
   Molasses Candy   28
A Family Reunion   31
   Sweet Tart Crust   32

Fruit Filling for Tarts   34
Jam Glaze   35
Demi and the Raisins   37
Plum Pudding   38

FROM
Little Men

Nat's Gingerbread   45
Gingerbread   46
Boston Brown Bread   47
Baked Apples   50
Nat's Steak and Potatoes   53
Steak   54
Potatoes   55
Asia's Gingersnaps   57
Gingersnaps   58
Daisy's Pies   61
Pie Crust   62
Apple Pie   65
Strawberry Pie   66
Tommy's Pattycakes   69
Pattycakes   70
Thanksgiving   73
Honey Pumpkin Pie in
Gingersnap Crust   74
Herbed Carrots   77
Candied Cranberries   78

References   80
Index of Recipes   81

To the Reader

The idea for this cookbook came to me while I was reading *Little Women*. Most of the foods mentioned throughout the novel sounded very appealing, especially since my hobby is cooking. So I began to wonder what it would be like to write and illustrate a cookbook based on the writings of Louisa May Alcott. After reading *Little Men*, I had enough material to begin.

First I researched recipes from cookbooks written in or about the late nineteenth century. Then I tested each recipe and chose the ones I thought tasted the best. Finally, I put the scenes from the novels together with the recipes I had chosen and coded each with a level of difficulty. The easiest recipes have one star; the most difficult have three.

I had a lot of fun compiling this cookbook, and I hope you will have fun using it. Happy cooking!

Gretchen Anderson
Sudbury, Massachusetts

Louisa May Alcott

Louisa May Alcott led an interesting but sometimes tragic life. When she was a girl, her father spent many years experimenting with philosophical ideas and projects, which often ended in failure.

Fruitlands, where the Alcotts had lived for nine months, was just one of those projects. Bronson Alcott and his colleagues knew a lot about philosophy, but little about farming. They tried to run the farm without ever slaughtering any animals. What few crops they grew were eaten by the hungry livestock. In his disappointment over Fruitlands' failure, Louisa's father fell ill. The family moved to Concord, Massachusetts, in an attempt to establish a normal life and nurse Bronson back to health.

A friend of Bronson, Ralph Waldo Emerson, gave much money to the struggling Alcotts while they lived in Concord. Mr. Alcott accepted these donations with his head held high, but Louisa was not able to do so. Therefore, as a way of repaying Mr. Emerson, she opened a school for all the little Emerson children.

Louisa had three sisters, Anna, Elizabeth, and May. The youngest, May, was forever trying to duplicate famous pictures. Her artistic attempts often amused the Alcott family.

Elizabeth was an angel, or so it seemed. She was reckless Louisa's comfort and companion. Her life was very short; at the age of twenty-three, gentle Beth died of scarlet fever. The Alcotts, in their grief, moved to a different house in Concord. They brought Elizabeth's piano and cherished it in her memory.

Anna, the oldest, enjoyed acting and being the elder sister. She married a kind and hardworking man, and gave birth to two little boys.

Louisa never married, and she led a full and active life. During the Civil War, she enlisted as a nurse and gave aid and comfort to many soldiers. This could not always keep them alive, however, and she saw many men die around her.

Louisa was brought home from war by her father when she fell ill. She never fully regained her health, but she was able to write. A man named Thomas Niles saw samples of her work and was delighted. He wanted her to write a "book for girls." So, in 1868, Louisa began *Little Women,* which was published the following year. It was a story based on her own life, each character representing someone she knew.

Although *Little Women* was a great success, the money and fame did little to improve Louisa's physical health. And in 1870, the Alcotts sent Louisa to Italy to recover. There she wrote *Little Men,* a sequel to *Little Women.* Louisa returned home, and for the next eighteen years she continued to write; she published a total of nine novels.

During this time, Louisa's illness worsened. By 1888, her

father, the only living member of the Alcott family, was dying, but Louisa was too weak to take care of him. While driving home from her last visit with him she caught a cold, which led to her death. She never knew that her father had died just before her.

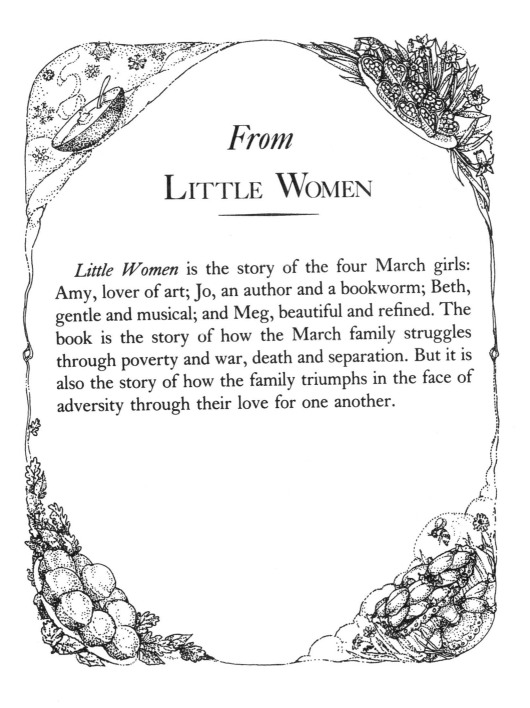

From

LITTLE WOMEN

Little Women is the story of the four March girls: Amy, lover of art; Jo, an author and a bookworm; Beth, gentle and musical; and Meg, beautiful and refined. The book is the story of how the March family struggles through poverty and war, death and separation. But it is also the story of how the family triumphs in the face of adversity through their love for one another.

The True Spirit of Christmas

It looked like a merry Christmas after all. Jo awoke on this special morning to find under her pillow a lovely crimson book of the story of Christmas. But, when the girls went downstairs, their dear Marmee was nowhere to be found. Hannah, the cook, informed them that their mother had gone to help a poor family. When Marmee returned, the March girls, with the true Christmas spirit, agreed to go back to the poor family and give them their breakfasts.

"May I go and help carry the things to the poor little children?" asked Beth eagerly.

"*I* shall take the cream and the muffins," added Amy, heroically giving up the articles she most liked.

Meg was already covering the buckwheats, and piling the bread into one big plate.

"I thought you'd do it," said Mrs. March, smiling as if satisfied. "You shall all go and help me, and when we come back we will have bread and milk for breakfast, and make it up at dinner-time."

They were soon ready, and the procession set out. Fortunately it was early, and they went through back streets, so few people saw them, and no one laughed at the queer party.

— LITTLE WOMEN

3

Anyone would be pleased to serve this breakfast, even if it weren't for Christmas.

Buckwheat Cakes

INGREDIENTS

2 cups very hot milk (scalded)
⅓ cup fine bread crumbs
¼ yeast cake
½ cup lukewarm water
½ teaspoon salt
Buckwheat flour
1 Tablespoon molasses
Butter

UTENSILS

Measuring cup
Small saucepan
Large mixing bowl
Measuring spoons
Large mixing spoon
Ladle
Griddle or frying pan
Spatula

METHOD   Difficulty**

1. The night before you wish to serve this, scald milk in small saucepan by heating it slowly until small bubbles form around the edge.
2. Pour the milk over the breadcrumbs in a large mixing bowl.
3. Let the breadcrumbs soak for 30 minutes.
4. Dissolve the yeast cake in lukewarm water.
5. To the breadcrumbs, add the yeast mixture, the salt, and

enough buckwheat flour to make a batter thin enough to pour.

6. Let this mixture rise overnight in a warm place.
7. Next morning, stir the batter and add the molasses.
8. Use a ladle to pour separate ladlefuls onto a hot griddle or frying pan greased with melted butter.

9. Cook until you see bubbles on the top of each cake.
10. Then use the spatula to turn each half-cooked cake and finish cooking by browning the other side.

SERVES 4 to 6.

Muffins

INGREDIENTS

3½ cups flour
5 teaspoons baking powder
1 teaspoon salt
3 Tablespoons sugar
1¾ cups milk
1 egg well beaten
3 Tablespoons melted butter
½ cup cranberries, dates, apples, berries, or nuts (optional)

UTENSILS

Measuring cups
Measuring spoons
Flour sifter
Large bowl
Mixing spoon
Muffin tins: 1 12-muffin pan plus 1 6-muffin pan or 3 6-muffin pans

METHOD   Difficulty*

1. Preheat oven to 350° and grease the muffin pans.
2. Sift dry ingredients (flour, baking powder, salt, and sugar) into large bowl.
3. Add the milk, egg, melted butter, and optional ingredient.
4. Stir until smooth.
5. Pour into greased muffin tins.
6. Bake for 25 minutes.

MAKES 18 MUFFINS.

Farina Gruel

INGREDIENTS

¾ cup farina
Cold water
2 cups boiling water
1 cup milk
1 egg well beaten

UTENSILS

Mixing bowls
Measuring spoons
Measuring cups
Mixing spoon
Heavy saucepan
Eggbeater

METHOD

Difficulty**

1. Make a thin paste by mixing the farina with some cold water.
2. Stir this paste into the boiling water and boil for 3–5 minutes. (Watch to see that it doesn't burn.)

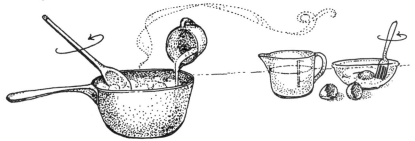

3. Next, add the milk and reheat.
4. Add a beaten egg to the gruel and heat until thickened.

SERVES 4–6.

A Gift from Mr. Laurence

When the March sisters put on a dramatic production for a group of girls at Christmas, a great surprise awaited them downstairs: a large assortment of bonbons, cake, ice cream, and fruit covered the table. In the middle, amid the sweets, were four bouquets of flowers!

This was a surprise, even to the actors; and, when they saw the table, they looked at one another in rapturous amazement. It was like Marmee to get up a little treat for them; but anything so fine as this was unheard-of since the departed days of plenty. There was ice-cream, — actually two dishes of it, pink and white, — and cake and fruit and distracting French bonbons, and, in the middle of the table, four great bouquets of hot-house flowers!

It quite took their breath away; and they stared first at the table and then at their mother, who looked as if she enjoyed it immensely.

"Is it fairies?" asked Amy.

"It's Santa Claus," said Beth.

"Mother did it;" and Meg smiled her sweetest, in spite of her gray beard and white eyebrows.

"Aunt March had a good fit, and sent the supper," cried Jo, with a sudden inspiration.

"All wrong. Old Mr. Laurence sent it," replied Mrs. March.

— LITTLE WOMEN

Bonbons

Mr. Laurence probably didn't make his own bonbons, but with this recipe and a little patience, you can make some that will taste a lot like his.

INGREDIENTS

⅓ *cup softened butter*
⅓ *cup light corn syrup*
½ *teaspoon salt*
1 *teaspoon vanilla extract*
4½ *cups sifted confectioner's sugar*
Flour (for kneading)
¼ *teaspoon lemon or orange extract (optional)*
A few drops food coloring (optional)

UTENSILS

Mixing bowl
Mixing spoon
Rolling pin
Cutting board
Small cookie cutters (if desired)

METHOD   Difficulty*

1. Mix all ingredients together, first with a spoon, then with your hands. (You may wish to add either lemon or orange extract for flavoring. You may also wish to divide the mixture into parts, which you can tint different colors.)

2. Put the mixture on a lightly floured cutting board and knead (turn over and over, pressing each time with the bottom of your hand) until smooth and well blended.

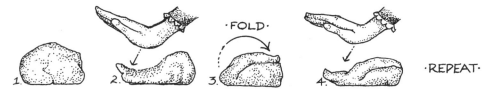

3. Shaping the bonbons can be done in several ways:
   a. You may roll the mixture into small balls.
   b. You may roll the mixture into thin strips and cut them into small log-shaped pieces.
   c. You may roll the mixture thin and cut it with cookie cutters.
4. Refrigerate until ready to serve.

MAKES 2 DOZEN BONBONS.

Pound Cake

Cakes come in many sizes, shapes, and flavors. A pound cake is a very basic cake, containing one pound of each ingredient. You may need some help to make it, but this cake will be worth the effort.

INGREDIENTS

4 sticks butter (1 pound)
2 cups granulated sugar (1 pound)
8 eggs
1 lemon
4 cups flour (1 pound)

UTENSILS

3 bowls
Eggbeater or electric mixer
Mixing spoon
Grater
Saucer
Measuring cup
Sifter
2 9"x5" Loaf pans
Cake tester or toothpick

METHOD   Difficulty***

1. Get out all the ingredients and let them sit for an hour.
2. Preheat oven to 350°.
3. In a large bowl, beat the butter until fluffy. Slowly beat in sugar until, when you dip in a spoon, the mixture is light and fluffy.

4. Beat the eggs in a separate bowl until light and foamy (about 3 minutes).
5. Add the eggs slowly to the butter-sugar mixture, beating all the while.
6. Grate the lemon rind into the saucer until you get enough to measure 1 teaspoon.

7. Add lemon rind to batter.
8. Sift the flour into the third bowl.
9. Gradually add the flour to the batter, stirring after every ½ cup. The batter will be very thick.
10. Spoon into ungreased pan. Bake for ½ hour at 350 °, then reduce heat 25 ° (to 325 °) and bake for another 30 minutes.
11. Insert a toothpick or cake tester (the Alcotts would have used a broom straw) into the center of the cake. If it comes out dry, the cake is done.

SERVES 8–10.

Mouth-watering Chocolate Glaze

If you want, you can top each slice of pound cake with Mouth-watering Chocolate Glaze and ice cream.

INGREDIENTS

2 Tablespoons butter
2 squares unsweetened choco-
    late
1½ cups confectioner's sugar
1 teaspoon vanilla
Boiling water

UTENSILS

Small saucepan
Measuring cups
Medium-sized bowl
Mixing spoon
Measuring spoons

METHOD   Difficulty**

1. In a small saucepan melt butter and chocolate over low heat.

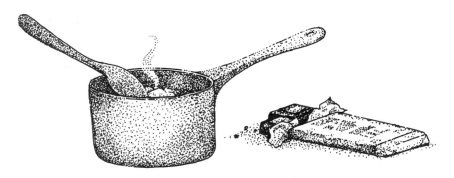

2. Put confectioner's sugar into a bowl. Slowly add the melted chocolate/butter mixture.
3. Mix until crumbly.
4. Add vanilla.

5. Carefully add boiling water one teaspoon at a time.
6. Stir constantly. Continue adding water until glaze is thin enough to pour.

The Pickwick Portfolio

During the summer, the girls created a club and published a club newsletter called *The Pickwick Portfolio*. Beth wrote a story for the paper and named it "The History of a Squash."

THE HISTORY OF A SQUASH

Once upon a time a farmer planted a little seed in his garden, and after a while it sprouted and became a vine, and bore many squashes. One day in October, when they were ripe, he picked one and took it to market. A grocerman bought and put it in his shop. That same morning, a little girl, in a brown hat and blue dress, with a round face and snub nose, went and bought it for her mother. She lugged it home, cut it up, and boiled it in the big pot; mashed some of it, with salt and butter, for dinner; and to the rest she added a pint of milk, two eggs, four spoons of sugar, nutmeg, and some crackers; put it in a deep dish, and baked it till it was brown and nice; and next day it was eaten by a family named March.

T. Tupman

— LITTLE WOMEN

Squash

Squash is a mild, delicious, nutritious vegetable, which is fast and simple to prepare.

INGREDIENTS

1 fairly large squash (summer variety)
Water
Salt
Butter
Brown sugar
Pepper
Cinnamon

UTENSILS

Knife
Large saucepan
Colander or large strainer
Bowl
Potato masher

METHOD   Difficulty*

1. Wash the squash and cut it into thick slices or cubes.

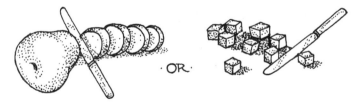

· OR ·

2. Fill a large saucepan half full of water and add a pinch of salt.
3. Let the water come to a boil and *carefully* add the squash. It is a good idea to turn off the flame and let the water settle before you add the squash.
4. Cook the squash for 15–20 minutes or until it is tender.

Test this by sticking a fork into a piece of squash. If it goes in easily, the squash is done.

5. Pour the squash into a colander and let it drain.
6. Put it into a bowl and mash it.

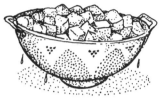

7. Add a little butter, salt, pepper, and brown sugar to season it. (A little cinnamon gives it a super flavor!)

Marmee's Breakfast

When Jo, Meg, Beth, and Amy had a week long vacation, they decided to spend it doing anything they pleased. After the first day, however, they were already bored, so they set about to prepare breakfast for their dear Marmee, who was sick in bed with a cold.

> The boiled tea was very bitter, the omelette scorched, and the biscuits speckled with saleratus; but Mrs. March received her repast with thanks, and laughed heartily over it after Jo was gone.

> — LITTLE WOMEN

Use caution while preparing these dishes or else you might have similar results.

Omelet

When you make an omelet be sure you choose one large egg for each person. Remember to use one tablespoon of liquid for each egg.

INGREDIENTS

4 eggs
½ teaspoon salt
Pepper
4 Tablespoons hot water
1 Tablespoon butter

UTENSILS

2 mixing bowls
Eggbeater or electric mixer
Measuring spoons
Rubber spatula
Frying pan or omelet pan

METHOD   Difficulty**

1. Carefully separate the egg yolks from the whites in separate bowls. (Crack each egg and use one shell to catch the yolk. Go back and forth in this manner until the whites are in the bowl and the yolks remain in the shell.) Then put the yolks into a second bowl.

2. Beat the egg yolks until they become thick and lemon-colored.
3. Add the salt, pepper, and hot water.
4. Beat the egg whites until they are stiff.
5. The next part is a little tricky! Fold the egg whites into the egg yolk mixture. Use a rubber spatula to help you turn the egg whites over and around in the yolk mixture.

4. REPEAT.

3. FLIP SPATULA UP & OVER.

1. SPATULA DOWN CENTER TO BOTTOM OF BOWL.

2. TURN BOWL HALFWAY.

6. Butter the sides and bottom of the omelet pan or frying pan, then heat the pan. WARNING: If you have a pan with wooden handles, *please* don't use it for this recipe! Putting it in the oven would be a big mistake.
7. Pour the mixture into the pan and spread it around evenly.
8. Let it cook slowly on the stove.
9. When it puffs up and browns a little on the bottom, put it into a slow (300°) oven to finish cooking, about 3 minutes.
10. It will feel firm when you touch it, if it is done.
11. Finally, take the omelet out of the oven and fold it in half to serve.

SERVES 4.

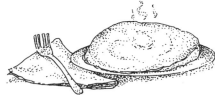

Baking Powder Biscuits

INGREDIENTS

2 cups flour
4 teaspoons baking powder
½ teaspoon salt
2 Tablespoons butter
¾ cup milk
Extra flour

UTENSILS

Large bowl
Flour sifter
Mixing spoon
Cutting board
Rolling pin
Biscuit cutter or drinking glass
Cookie sheet

METHOD   Difficulty**

1. Preheat oven to 400°.
2. Grease a cookie sheet.
3. Combine the dry ingredients (flour, baking powder, and salt).
4. Sift them together twice.

5. Work in the butter with your fingertips.
6. Slowly add the milk and mix to a soft dough.
7. Cover the cutting board with the extra flour.
8. Roll out the dough until it is about ½ inch thick.
9. Cut with a biscuit cutter (or the top of a drinking glass, dipped in flour).

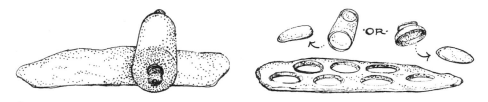

10. Put the biscuits on a greased cookie sheet and bake 12–15 minutes or until golden brown.

MAKES 12–15 BISCUITS.

Jo's Dinner Party

Jo was feeling ambitious. Her imagination was on the run again. She was going to have a dinner party. Jo's faith in herself, however, was stretched a bit too far. To Meg's horror, Jo was going to invite Laurie, the rich boy next door, to dine with her.

> "You'd better see what you have got before you think of having company," said Meg, when informed of the hospitable but rash act.
>
> "Oh, there's corned beef and plenty of potatoes; and I shall get some asparagus, and a lobster, 'for a relish,' as Hannah says. We'll have lettuce, and make a salad. I don't know how, but the book tells. I'll have blanc-mange and strawberries for dessert; and coffee, too, if you want to be elegant."
>
> "Don't try too many messes, Jo, for you can't make anything but gingerbread and molasses candy, fit to eat. I wash my hands of the dinner-party; and, since you have asked Laurie on your own responsibility, you may just take care of him."
>
> — LITTLE WOMEN

Jo's dinner was a failure. Had she stuck to what she knew, the dinner might have been a sweet success.

Molasses Candy

A friendly tip: be sure to do this on a cool dry day (not in July in the middle of a humid spell)!

INGREDIENTS

3 Tablespoons butter
2 cups molasses
⅔ cups sugar
Water
1 Tablespoon vinegar

UTENSILS

Heavy saucepan
Measuring cups
Mixing spoon
Measuring spoons
12" x 16" x 2" pan (or cookie sheet with sides), heavily buttered
Sharp knife
Waxed paper

METHOD   Difficulty***

1. Butter the pan heavily.
2. Melt butter in a heavy saucepan.
3. Add the molasses and the sugar.
4. Stir until the sugar is dissolved. Use a wooden spoon.
5. Continue to boil and stir until you test to see if it is done. Do so by dropping a small amount of the mixture into cold water. The candy is ready when it becomes brittle (hard) in the water. You can also test it by checking to see if it reads 256° on a candy thermometer.

6. Just before you remove the pan from the fire, add the vinegar slowly. THIS STEP CAN BE DIFFICULT, SO BE CAREFUL. STAND AWAY FROM THE PAN WHEN YOU ADD THE VINEGAR.
7. Pour the mixture into the pan.
8. Wait a while (up to 1 hour). When the candy is cool enough to handle, grease your hands lightly, and keep spare shortening handy. Pull it (using the tips of your fingers) until it becomes golden in color and shiny. NOTE: You may have to pull for 15 minutes. Also, if you pull and fold and pull again, it is easier to handle.

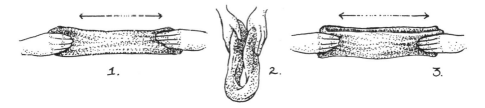

9. Cool candy on lightly buttered dishes.
10. Finally, roll candy into a snake-like shape, ½ inch thick.
11. Cut into two-inch pieces with a sharp buttered knife or kitchen scissors (be careful; you might need some help from an adult) and wrap each in waxed paper.

MAKES ABOUT 1½ POUNDS.

A Family Reunion

When the March family gathered to celebrate Amy and Laurie's marriage, everyone was so excited that they all began talking at once. Meg's twins, Daisy and Demi, were happy to be ignored, because they could do as they pleased.

The twins pranced behind, feeling that the millennium was at hand, for every one was so busy with the newcomers that they were left to revel at their own sweet will, and you may be sure they made the most of the opportunity. Didn't they steal sips of tea, stuff gingerbread *ad libitum,* get a hot biscuit apiece, and, as a crowning trespass, didn't they each whisk a captivating little tart into their tiny pockets, there to stick and crumble treacherously, teaching them that both human nature and pastry are frail? Burdened with the guilty consciousness of the sequestered tarts, and fearing that Dodo's sharp eyes would pierce the thin disguise of cambric and merino which hid their booty, the little sinners attached themselves to "Dranpa," who hadn't his spectacles on.

— LITTLE WOMEN

31

Sweet Tart Crust

When you try these delicious tarts, you too may wish to sequester some for a late night snack.

INGREDIENTS

1½ cup flour
¼ cup fine granulated sugar
½ teaspoon salt
1¼ sticks (½ cup plus 2 Tablespoons) butter
2 egg yolks
1 teaspoon vanilla
2 teaspoons cold water

UTENSILS

Measuring cups
Measuring spoons
Sifter
2 mixing bowls
Fork (or pastry blender)
Cutting board
Rolling pin
Waxed paper
Large round cookie cutter
Muffin tins or tart pans

METHOD   **Difficulty*****

1. Sift dry ingredients (flour, sugar, and salt) into mixing bowl.
2. Cut chilled butter into flour mixture with the fork. Then rub the butter and flour together with your fingertips until the mixture looks like a lot of tiny crumbs.

3. Mix egg yolks, vanilla, and water together, then add it to the flour-butter mixture using a fork, or pastry blender.
4. Quickly shape the dough into a ball.
5. Put the dough on a board and break off ¼ of it. With your palm, smear the dough away from you into a 6–8-inch circle. Repeat this with all of the dough. Then gather each quarter of the dough together into a ball, wrap in waxed paper, and refrigerate for 2 to 3 hours.
6. Preheat oven to 425°.
7. Roll out the dough between two pieces of waxed paper until it is about ½ inch thick. Cut out circles with a large round cutter.

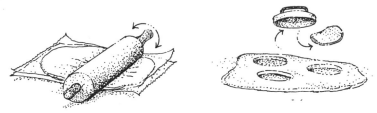

8. Place cutout shapes into greased muffin tins. Gently press the dough into the bottom and sides of each cup.
9. With a fork, carefully prick holes into the bottom and sides of each cup.
10. Bake at 425° for 8–10 minutes or until the edges are lightly browned.

MAKES 12 TART SHELLS.

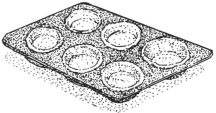

33

Fruit Filling for Tarts

You may wish to fill your tarts with any of the fruits or berries listed below.

INGREDIENTS

Strawberries
Blueberries
Raspberries
Cherries
Peach slices
Blackberries

UTENSILS

Knife, peeler, or strawberry huller

METHOD

1. Wash fruit.
2. If you are using strawberries, cut off green stems.
3. If you are using cherries, cut them in half and remove the pits.
4. If you are using peaches, peel them, then remove the pits and slice them thinly.
5. Place enough fruit in the tart shells to fill to the top.
6. Pour glaze over the top.

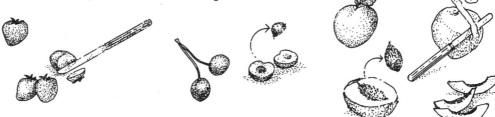

Jam Glaze

The following jams may be used for glazes:

INGREDIENTS

Raspberry
Red currant
Strawberry
(*Or your favorite jam or jelly*)

UTENSILS

Small saucepan
Spoon
Pastry brush

METHOD

1. Melt 1 cup of jam in a small saucepan over very low heat.
2. Carefully spoon a small amount of jam over the fruit in each tart.
3. You may wish to brush some extra jam on top of the berries with a pastry brush.

MAKES 12 TARTS.

Demi and the Raisins

One day Meg was making plum pudding, and Demi was eating all the raisins:

"No more raisins, Demi, they'll make you sick," says mamma to the young person, who offers his services in the kitchen with unfailing regularity on plum-pudding day.

"Me likes to be sick."

"I don't want to have you, so run away and help Daisy make patty-cakes."

He reluctantly departs, but his wrongs weigh upon his spirit; and, by and by, when an opportunity comes to redress them, he outwits mamma by a shrewd bargain.

"Now you have been good children, and I'll play anything you like," says Meg, as she leads her assistant cooks upstairs, when the pudding is safely bouncing in the pot.

"Truly marmar?" asks Demi, with a brilliant idea in his well-powdered head.

"Yes, truly; anything you say," replies the short-sighted parent, preparing herself to sing "The Three Little Kittens" half a dozen times over, or to take her family to "Buy a penny bun," regardless of wind or limb. But Demi corners her by the cool reply, —

"Then we'll go and eat up all the raisins."

— LITTLE WOMEN

37

Plum Pudding

Though somewhat difficult to make, this pudding is delicious warm on a cold day. But, don't eat all the raisins!

INGREDIENTS

1 cup stale breadcrumbs
1 cup very hot milk (scalded)
4 eggs
½ cup sugar
1 cup raisins (cut them into pieces and roll them in flour)
½ cup currants
½ cup figs, chopped into very small pieces
2 ounces citron (cut into tiny pieces)
½ pound suet
¼ cup brandy (ask for help with this)
½ teaspoon nutmeg
¾ teaspoon cinnamon
¼ teaspoon ground cloves
¼ teaspoon mace

UTENSILS

Mixing bowls
Measuring spoons
Measuring cups
Electric mixer or wooden spoon
Kitchen knife
Pudding mold or clean, one-pound coffee tin
Cake or roasting rack
Large kettle or pot for steaming
Flat-bladed table knife

Method

Difficulty***

1. Soak the breadcrumbs in milk and put them aside until they cool.
2. Separate the egg yolks from the egg whites.

3. Beat the yolks and add them to the cooled breadcrumbs along with the sugar, raisins, currants, figs, and citron.
4. Chop the suet and mix it until it is creamy. (Cooks used to use their hands to do this!)

5. Beat the egg whites until stiff, and set aside.

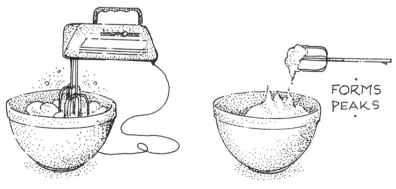

FORMS PEAKS

6. Combine the suet with the breadcrumb mixture.
7. Add the brandy, nutmeg, cinnamon, cloves, mace, and the beaten egg whites.
8. Pour the mixture into a buttered mold or coffee tin and cover (aluminum foil can be used for the tin).

9. Place the mold on a rack in a large kettle.

10. Pour boiling water into the kettle to 1″ deep; cover the kettle.

11. Steam for 6 hours or until done, adding more boiling water if necessary.
12. Carefully remove the mold from the kettle and allow to cool for 10 minutes.
13. Unmold the pudding. Slide the blade of a dull table knife down inside the mold or can, and gently loosen the pudding until it no longer sticks to the mold. Tip the pudding out onto a plate, sideways, then put it right-side-up. It can be sliced by tightening a loop of string around it. You may then want to divide these circular slices into halves or quarters with a knife, since the pudding is very rich.

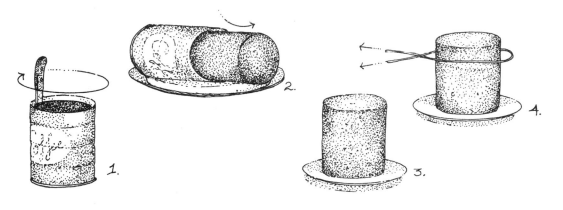

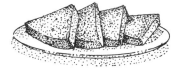

From

LITTLE MEN

Little Men, a sequel to *Little Women,* is the story of the good and bad times at Plumfield, Jo's school for boys. Jo and her husband, Professor Bhaer, created a recipe for a successful school: a few cupfuls of rich, wrongly treated boys; one or two ragamuffins; a nurse for bruises and bumps; a reckless, motherless little girl; and — to spice up life — a lot of love.

Nat's Gingerbread

Nat, a poor ragamuffin, was sent to Plumfield by a rich, kind man named Mr. Laurence. A pretty, merry-faced maid answered the door when Nat arrived and invited him in. A large household filled with children was immediately presented before his eyes — quite a scene to behold!

In the room on the left a long supper-table was seen, set forth with great pitchers of new milk, piles of brown and white bread, and perfect stacks of the shiny gingerbread so dear to boyish souls. A flavor of toast was in the air, also suggestions of baked apples, very tantalizing to one hungry little nose and stomach.

— LITTLE MEN

Gingerbread

This is a very good recipe for gingerbread. I prefer it for dessert with whipped cream.

INGREDIENTS

1½ cups white flour
1 teaspoon baking soda
½ teaspoon salt
½ teaspoon ginger
1 teaspoon cinnamon
¼ cup vegetable oil
¼ cup maple syrup
¼ cup honey
½ cup yogurt
1 large egg, slightly beaten

UTENSILS

Measuring cups
Measuring spoons
Flour sifter
Fork
Large mixing bowl
Electric mixer
8" square pan
Cake tester or toothpick

METHOD   Difficulty**

1. Preheat oven to 350°.
2. Sift dry ingredients (flour, baking soda, salt, ginger, and cinnamon) into a large mixing bowl. Mix well with a fork.
3. Pour liquid ingredients (oil, maple sugar, honey, yogurt, and egg) into a 2-cup measure. Mix well.
4. Mix dry and wet ingredients.
5. Pour into the square pan.

6. Bake for 30–35 minutes.

7. When the time is up, insert a cake tester or toothpick into the center of the gingerbread. If the tester is clean when you remove it, then the gingerbread is done.

MAKES 16 SQUARES.

Boston Brown Bread

Now here is an old-fashioned recipe for Boston Brown Bread. It's a little difficult to make, but I think you'll regard it as worth the effort.

INGREDIENTS

1 cup rye flour
1 cup cornmeal
1 cup graham flour
¾ Tablespoon baking soda
1 teaspoon salt
¾ cup dark molasses
1¾ cups milk
Butter
Boiling water

UTENSILS

Measuring cup
Measuring spoons
Flour sifter
Large mixing bowl
Electric mixer or spoon
3 empty 1-pound coffee cans
Aluminum foil
Wire rack
Deep pan large enough to hold coffee cans
1 table knife

METHOD   Difficulty***

1. Sift dry ingredients (rye flour, cornmeal, graham flour, baking soda, and salt) into a large bowl.

2. Add molasses and milk and mix until well blended.
3. Butter the coffee cans.
4. Half-fill the coffee cans with batter. Cover tightly with aluminum foil.

BATTER

FOIL

5. Place the rack inside the pan. Place cans on rack and pour boiling water into the pan so that it comes halfway up the cans.

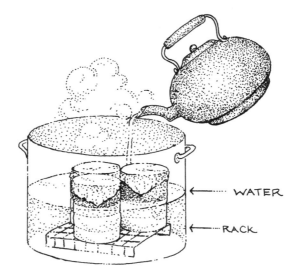

WATER

RACK

6. Cover the pan tightly with aluminum foil (or a cover), place on the stove, and steam for 3 hours.
7. Preheat the oven to 300°.
8. Uncover the cans and bake the bread in the oven for 15 minutes. Then remove the bread from the cans. Slide the blade of a dull table knife straight down inside can at the edge of the bread. Gently move the upright knife all the way around the can, to loosen any part that sticks. Then turn each can upside down on a plate, slapping the bottom to release the brown bread. Lay the bread on its side to cut it.

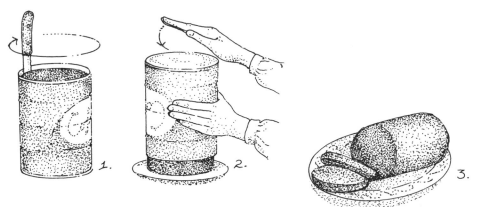

MAKES 3 CYLINDRICAL LOAVES.

Baked Apples

I absolutely *love* them!

INGREDIENTS

6 big apples
6–12 Tablespoons brown
    sugar
1½ teaspoon cinnamon
6 teaspoons butter
1 cup water
Optional additions:
    coconut
    granola
    cranberries
    nuts
    cinnamon candies

UTENSILS

Apple peeler and corer or
    paring knife
Baking dish
Measuring spoons
Measuring cup

METHOD   Difficulty**

1. Core apples. (Stick pointed side of corer into stem area.
   Gently twist corer down until you nearly reach the bottom
   of the apple. Slowly remove the core.)

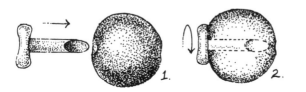 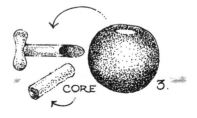

2. Using the peeler or paring knife, remove a 1″ strip around the top of each apple.

3. Place apples upright in baking dish.

4. Fill each apple with 1–2 Tablespoons of brown sugar mixed with ¼ teaspoon cinnamon and 1 teaspoon of butter.
5. You may wish to add other ingredients from the choices listed above.
6. Pour 1 cup of water around apples.

7. Bake at 375° for 45–60 minutes. Carefully spoon juices over apples every 15 minutes or so.

SERVES 6.

51

Nat's Steak and Potatoes

When Nat woke on the Sunday of his first day in Plumfield, he found a clean suit of clothes on the chair beside his bed. When he was dressed, he went downstairs to discover that all the other pupils were lined up neatly beside their chairs.

> The sun was shining into the dining-room on the well-spread table, and the flock of hungry, hearty lads who gathered round it. Nat observed that they were much more orderly than they had been the night before, and every one stood silently behind his chair while little Rob, standing beside his father at the head of the table, folded his hands, reverently bent his curly head, and softly repeated a short grace in the devout German fashion, which Mr. Bhaer loved and taught his little son to honor. Then they all sat down to enjoy the Sunday-morning breakfast of coffee, steak, and baked potatoes, instead of the bread and milk fare with which they usually satisfied their young appetites.
>
> — LITTLE MEN

You'll have to get up pretty early to make this, or else have it for a special brunch. But it's worth it!

Steak

INGREDIENTS

Small steaks (¼–½ pound each), suitable for broiling
Mustard (sweet or spicy, depending on your taste)

UTENSILS

Cookie sheet
Sharp knife
Fork to turn steak

METHOD   **Difficulty***

1. Heat the stove broiler.
2. Spread a little mustard thinly on one side of each steak.
3. Put the steaks on a cookie sheet and broil 2 to 3 inches from the broiler, about 7 minutes.
4. Turn the steak, spread more mustard, and broil another 7 minutes, or until done.
5. Check for doneness by cutting into the steak. If you like it rare, cook until pink inside; cook slightly longer for medium or well done.

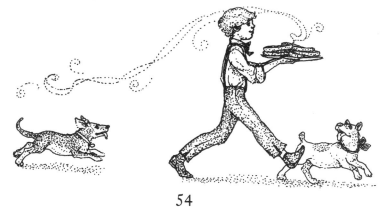

Potatoes

INGREDIENTS

One medium-sized potato per person
Butter or sour cream

UTENSILS

Cookie sheet
Fork

METHOD   **Difficulty***

1. Heat oven to 375°.
2. Scrub the potatoes and poke holes in both ends so they won't explode.

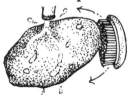 

3. Place potatoes on a cookie sheet in oven for an hour or until a fork goes into them easily, but they are not mushy.
4. Serve with butter or sour cream.

Asia's Gingersnaps

On a hot summer day at Plumfield, Daisy came into the house complaining because the boys would not allow her to play football. Her Aunt Jo, who had plenty of work to do, sent her to see what Asia, the cook, had for lunch.

In five minutes Daisy was back again, with a wide-awake face, a bit of dough in her hand and a dab of flour on her little nose.

"O Aunty! please could I go and make gingersnaps and things? Asia isn't cross, and she says I may, and it would be such fun, please do," cried Daisy, all in one breath.

— LITTLE MEN

Daisy was permitted to go and her cookies came out beautifully. Yours will, too, with this delicious recipe.

Gingersnaps

INGREDIENTS

1 cup molasses
½ cup butter
3¼ cups flour
2 cups brown sugar
½ teaspoon baking soda
1 Tablespoon ginger
½ teaspoon cinnamon
¼ teaspoon ground cloves
Extra flour

UTENSILS

Measuring cups
Measuring spoons
Small saucepan
Mixing spoon
Large bowl
Flour sifter
Small bowl
Cutting board or surface for
*   rolling out dough*
Rolling pin
Round cookie cutter
Cookie sheet(s)

METHOD   Difficulty***

1. Heat the molasses until it boils. Be careful.
2. Pour the molasses over the butter in a bowl. NOTE: Please don't use a plastic bowl! It could be melted by the hot molasses.
3. Sift the dry ingredients (flour, sugar, baking soda, and spices) into a small bowl.

4. Gradually add the dry ingredients to the molasses mixture. Stir well.
5. Chill this dough for several hours.
6. Preheat oven to 350°.
7. Cover a cutting board with flour.
8. Divide the dough into four pieces. Keep the pieces you are not using in a cool place.
9. Roll out each piece as thin as possible. Keep the rolling pin well floured.
10. Cut out cookies with floured round cutter.

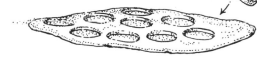

11. Put the cookies on a greased cookie sheet and bake until done (about 10 minutes).
   NOTE: As you cut out the cookies you will have many scraps of dough left over. Just add these to the remaining dough.

MAKES 4 DOZEN.

Daisy's Pies

Aunt Jo told Daisy that she would find her something new to play with, but what a something! When Daisy was finally permitted to see it, she found a cast iron stove, just her size, that really worked. Daisy was eager to start making her own dinner immediately.

"Am I going to have pie?" cried Daisy, hardly believing that such bliss could be in store for her.

"Yes; if your oven does well we will have two pies, — one apple and one strawberry," said Mrs. Jo, who was nearly as much interested in the new play as Daisy herself. . . .

Daisy got things together with as little noise and spilling as could be expected, from so young a cook.

"I really don't know how to measure for such tiny pies; I must guess at it, and if these don't succeed, we must try again," said Mrs. Jo, looking rather perplexed, and very much amused with the small concern before her. "Take that little pan full of flour, put in a pinch of salt, and then rub in as much butter as will go on that plate. Always remember to put your dry things together first, and then the wet. It mixes better so."

"I know how; I saw Asia do it. Don't I butter the pie plates too? She did, the first thing," said Daisy, whisking the flour about at a great rate.

"Quite right! I do believe you have a gift for cooking, you take to it so cleverly," said Aunt Jo, approvingly.

— LITTLE MEN

Although Daisy's pies were miniature, these recipes will make delicious, tasty, people-sized apple and strawberry pies.

Pie Crust

INGREDIENTS

2½ cups flour
⅔ cups lard (or other solid shortening)
5–7 Tablespoons ice water or apple juice
Extra flour
2 Tablespoons butter
2 Tablespoons sugar

UTENSILS

Measuring cups
Measuring spoons
Large bowl
Fork
Waxed paper
Rolling pin
8" or 9" pie plate

METHOD   Difficulty***

1. Put the flour into a large bowl.
2. Add the lard and, with a fork, mix the lard into the flour until there are rough-looking pieces.
3. Slowly add the liquid, mixing it with the fork.
4. Dip your hands in flour and gather and press the mixture until it forms a dough.
5. If the dough is very sticky, add a *little* more flour. If the dough is too flaky, add a little more liquid. *Be careful!*

6. Wipe a tabletop or countertop with a damp cloth.

7. Place a large sheet of waxed paper on the surface. (The waxed paper will stick to the wet surface.)

8. Take the dough from the bowl, divide the dough in half, and place it on the waxed paper.

9. On top of that put a second piece of waxed paper (like a sandwich).

10. Rub a handful of flour on the rolling pin.

11. Roll out half of the dough, keeping it sandwiched between the sheets of waxed paper. When finished, the crust should be about ¼″ thick.

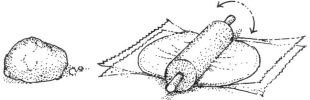

12. Hold the pie plate over the flattened dough. If you have rolled it enough, some crust will peep out (about 1½″) beyond the rim of the pie plate. If it doesn't, roll some more, leaning a little harder.

13. *Here's the hard part.* Peel the top piece of waxed paper from the crust. Place one hand on the bare dough, and your other hand on the underside of the paper. KEEP THE BOTTOM PIECE OF WAXED PAPER ON.

14. Flip the crust, bare side down, into the pie plate.

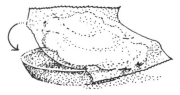 

15. Peel off the bottom waxed paper. Press the dough gently into the bottom of the pie plate and up the sides.
16. Roll out the second half of the dough, following the above steps, but don't put it into the pie plate just yet.
17. Pour in apple filling (see following recipe). Place small pieces of butter on top of filling.
18. Take your second crust, peel off one piece of waxed paper, and place the crust bare side down on the filling.
19. Peel off the last piece of waxed paper.
20. Take the two edges of the two crusts and pinch them together all the way around. Make sure it is well sealed; wetting the top edge of the bottom crust helps.

21. Make three slits in the top crust with a knife.
22. Sprinkle the crust with sugar.
23. Follow baking instructions for apple pie.

MAKES AN 8″ OR 9″ PIE.

Apple Pie

INGREDIENTS

7 apples
¾ cup sugar
2 Tablespoons flour
1 teaspoon cinnamon
⅛ teaspoon ground cloves
⅛ teaspoon nutmeg
Pie crust (see recipe on page 62)

UTENSILS

Measuring cups
Measuring spoons
Large mixing bowls
Large spoon
Rolling pin
8" or 9" pie plate
Fork
Potato or apple peeler
Sharp knife

METHOD   Difficulty***

1. Preheat oven to 400°.
2. Roll out half the amount of pie dough (page 63) and fit into an 8" or 9" pie plate.
3. Take a fork and make little holes in the pie crust. This prevents it from shrinking.
4. Peel, core, and slice the apples thin.
5. In the bowl combine sugar, flour, cinnamon, cloves, and nutmeg.
6. Add the apples and lightly mix until all the apples are covered.
7. Pour apples into prepared bottom crust.
8. Cover with top crust (see page 64) and bake at 400° for 50 minutes.

SERVES 8.

Strawberry Pie

INGREDIENTS

*1 baked pie shell (Use half of
  the recipe on page 62).*
3–4 cups large strawberries
*½–1 cup strawberry jam or
  red currant jam*

UTENSILS

Rolling pin
8" or 9" pie plate
Fork
Measuring cup
Large strainer
*Small knife or strawberry
  huller*
Small saucepan
Pastry brush

METHOD   Difficulty*

1. Preheat oven to 450°.
2. Roll out half the amount of pie dough (pages 62–63) and
   fit into the pie plate.
3. Take a fork and make little holes in the pie crust. (This
   prevents it from shrinking.) Bake the pie shell until it is
   golden in color (about 10–12 minutes). Let it cool.
4. Place the strawberries in the strainer and allow cold water
   to run gently on them.

5. Using the knife or the huller, remove green stems from the strawberries.

6. Place the strawberries, pointed side up, in the pie shell.

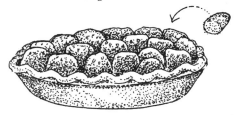

7. Melt the jam in the saucepan over a *low* heat.

8. Pour the melted jam over the strawberries. *Be careful!*

9. Using the pastry brush, lightly brush the strawberries with the jam.

10. You may refrigerate the pie if you wish.

SERVES 8.

Tommy's Pattycakes

When Nan, a wild, naughty little girl, and Daisy, her sweet and polite playmate, held a party with the boys, there was trouble brewing.

The best pie flew wildly on the floor when [Daisy] tried to cut it with a very dull knife; the bread and butter vanished with a rapidity calculated to dismay a housekeeper's soul; and, worst of all, the custards were so soft that they had to be drunk up, instead of being eaten elegantly with the new tin spoons.

I grieve to state that [Nan] squabbled with the maid for the best jumble, which caused Bess to toss the whole dish into the air, and burst out crying amid a rain of falling cakes. She was comforted by a seat at the table, and the sugar-bowl to empty; but during this flurry a large plate of patties was mysteriously lost, and could not be found. They were the chief ornament of the feast, and Mrs. Smith was indignant at the loss, for she had made them herself, and they were beautiful to behold. I put it to any lady if it was not hard to have one dozen delicious patties (made of flour, salt, and water, with a large raisin in the middle of each, and much sugar over the whole) swept away at one fell swoop?

— LITTLE MEN

69

Pattycakes

This recipe makes a different type of pattycake from the one described, but it is very good nevertheless.

INGREDIENTS

4 cups flour
1 teaspoon cream of tartar
1½ cups sugar
¾ cups soft butter
2 eggs
1 teaspoon vanilla
½ teaspoon almond extract, or
1 teaspoon grated orange or lemon rind
½ teaspoon baking soda
½ cup sour cream
1 egg yolk, beaten
Extra flour
Extra sugar, cinnamon, nutmeg, ginger

UTENSILS

Measuring cup
Measuring spoons
Sifter
Large, medium, and small bowls
Eggbeater or electric mixer
Cheese grater
Cutting board
Rolling pin
Cookie cutters
Cookie sheet
Pastry brush

METHOD   Difficulty***

1. Sift together flour and cream of tartar.
2. Beat the butter until creamy. Slowly add the sugar, a little

at a time. Cream the butter and sugar until the mixture is light and fluffy.

3. Gradually beat in eggs, vanilla, almond extract, or lemon rind, or orange rind. The rind can be either bought or grated by you with a cheese grater. To grate it: Hold the lemon in one hand and the grater, over a plate or clean counter top, in the other. Rub the lemon against the grating side. The rind will fall onto the plate.

4. Dissolve the baking soda in sour cream.

5. Add the flour mixture and sour cream mixture to the creamed butter and sugar in this way. First, add about ⅓ of the flour mixture and blend well. Then add ½ of the sour cream mixture and mix well. Repeat these steps, ending with the flour mixture.

6. Chill dough for several hours, or overnight.

7. Preheat oven to 350°.

8. Roll out on a cutting board about a third of the dough at a time to a thickness of ¼ inch. (Be sure to flour the cutting board well first.)

9. Cut out cookies and place them on a greased cookie sheet.

10. Brush the cookies with beaten egg yolk and sprinkle lavishly with extra sugar, or a mixture of sugar, cinnamon, nutmeg, and ginger.

11. Bake for about 15 minutes. Do not overbake.

MAKES 6 DOZEN.

Thanksgiving

At Plumfield, Thanksgiving was quite a lively occasion. Days and days were spent baking and stewing. Odors filled the air — enough to make a stomach feel as hollow as a balloon.

For days beforehand, the little girls helped Asia and Mrs. Jo in store-room and kitchen, making pies and puddings, sorting fruit, dusting dishes, and being very busy and immensely important. The boys hovered on the outskirts of the forbidden ground, sniffing the savory odors, peeping in at the mysterious performances, and occasionally being permitted to taste some delicacy in the process of preparation.

— LITTLE MEN

You don't have to wait until Thanksgiving to enjoy these delectable treats. They can be made any time of year.

Honey Pumpkin Pie
in Gingersnap Crust

Gingersnap Crust

INGREDIENTS

2 cups crushed gingersnaps
(see page 58)
⅓ cup softened butter

UTENSILS

Waxed paper
Rolling pin
2-cup measure
Bowl
9" pie plate

METHOD   **Difficulty*****

1. Tear off two fairly large sheets of waxed paper.
2. Place about 12 cookies on one piece of waxed paper. Cover with the second sheet.
3. Crush cookies by rolling back and forth with the rolling pin.

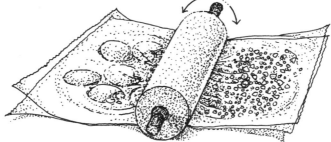

4. Put crushed cookies into the measuring cup. Repeat until you have two cups of crumbs.

5. In a medium-sized bowl, mix the crumbs with the butter (fingers work well).
6. Press mixture into the bottom and sides of a buttered pie plate.

Honey Pumpkin Pie Filling

INGREDIENTS

2 cups canned pumpkin
½ cup sugar
½ cup brown sugar
1½ teaspoon cinnamon
½ teaspoon ginger
½ teaspoon nutmeg
⅓ cup honey
1 cup evaporated milk
2 eggs, slightly beaten
1 gingersnap pie crust

UTENSILS

Large mixing bowl
Large wooden spoon
Measuring cups
Measuring spoons
Knife
Aluminum foil

METHOD   Difficulty**

1. Preheat oven to 400°.
2. Mix pumpkin with sugar, spices (cinnamon, ginger, and nutmeg), and honey in a large bowl.

3. Add milk and eggs. Blend the mixture well.
4. Carefully pour the mixture into an unbaked gingersnap crust.
5. Bake for about 50 minutes. Here's how to test for doneness. Take a clean knife. Gently stick it into the center of the pie. If it comes out clean, the pie is done.

6. CAUTION: The edges of the pie crust may cook faster than the rest of the pie. Check to see if this is happening. If it is, cover the edges with foil.

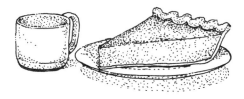

SERVES 8.

Herbed Carrots

INGREDIENTS

4 cups carrots
2 Tablespoons butter
2 Tablespoons water
1 teaspoon sugar
Parsley
Tarragon or rosemary or
  thyme (or your favorite
  herb)

UTENSILS

Carrot scraper (or serrated
  knife)
Measuring cups
Measuring spoons
Heavy saucepan with a cover

METHOD   Difficulty**

1. Wash, scrape, and cut into quarters enough carrots to make four cups.

2. Put the butter, water, and sugar in a heavy saucepan.
3. Add the carrots.
4. Cover tightly and cook over a low heat for 15–20 minutes.
5. Empty contents of saucepan into a bowl and season with bits of parsley and your favorite herbs to taste.

Candied Cranberries

Ingredients

2½ cups sugar
1½ cups water
1 quart cranberries

Utensils

Measuring cups
Heavy saucepan
Mixing spoon
Heat-proof bowl
Rack (cake or roasting)
Large kettle, pot, or steamer
    with cover
Canning or jelly jars

Method   Difficulty***

1. Mix sugar with water in a heavy saucepan.
2. Stir to dissolve sugar.
3. Bring to a boil.
4. Pour syrup over cranberries in a heat-proof bowl.
5. Put the bowl on a rack that has been placed in a large kettle, pot, or steamer.
6. Pour boiling water into pot to a depth of about 2″ (don't let water reach the sides of the bowl).

INSIDE VIEW ···⟶

WATER ···⟶
RACK ···⟶

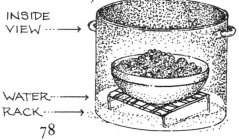

78

7. Cover and steam for 45 minutes over simmering water.

8. Carefully remove the bowl and cool the cranberries. Do not stir.

9. Let the cranberries stand in a warm, dry place for 3–4 days. Stir the mixture once or twice a day, until the syrup becomes jellylike.

10. Wash the jelly jars carefully and rinse with boiling water. If you have a dishwasher, wash them in that, and remove them (carefully) immediately. You may wish to ask for help from an adult.

11. Pour the cranberry mixture in the jars. Leave about an inch of space at the top. Tightly seal jars and store in the refrigerator.

    NOTE: Candied Cranberries make a nice gift!

References

Alcott, Abigail May, *Abigail May Alcott's Receipts and Simple Remedies,* Concord, Mass: Nancy L. Kohl and the Louisa May Alcott Memorial Association, 1980.

Alcott, Louisa May, *Little Men,* Boston: Little, Brown, 1901.

Alcott, Louisa May, *Little Women,* Boston: Little, Brown, 1915.

Berquist, Edna Smith, *The High Maples Farm Cookbook,* Boston: Houghton Mifflin, 1971.

Better Homes and Gardens Cookbook, Des Moines: Meredith Corporation, 1981.

Farmer, Fannie Merritt, *The Original Boston Cooking School Cookbook,* New York: Weathervane Books, 1896.

Kent, Louise Andrews, *The Vermont Year Round Cookbook,* Boston: Houghton Mifflin, 1965.

Meigs, Cornelia, *Invincible Louisa,* Boston: Little, Brown, 1933.

Walker, Barbara M., *The Little House Cookbook: Frontier Foods from Laura Ingalls' Classic Stories,* New York: Harper & Row, 1979.

Index of Recipes

Apple Pie 65

Baked Apples 50
Baking Powder Biscuits 24
Bonbons 10
Boston Brown Bread 47
Buckwheat Cakes 4

Candied Cranberries 78
Chocolate Glaze 14

Farina Gruel 7
Fruit Filling for Tarts 34

Gingerbread 46
Gingersnaps 58
Gingersnap Crust 74

Herbed Carrots 77
Honey Pumpkin Pie 74

Jam Glaze 35

Molasses Candy 28
Muffins 6

Omelet 22

Pattycakes 70
Pie Crust 62
Plum Pudding 38
Potatoes 55
Pound Cake 12

Squash 18
Steak 54
Strawberry Pie 66
Sweet Tart Crust 32